I0473801

Leading a Team

First Published 2012

ISBN-13: 978-1478332039
ISBN-10: 1478332034

Derek Good
Auckland
New Zealand

Copyright © 2012 Derek Good

All rights reserved. No part of this publication
may be reproduced, stored in a retrieval
system or transmitted in any form or by
any means, electronic, mechanical,
photocopying, recording or otherwise,
without the prior written permission of the author.

"You get the best effort from others not by lighting a fire beneath them, but by building a fire within."

- Bob Nelson

Contents

"Leaders manage the dream. All leaders have the capacity to create a compelling vision, one that takes people to a new place, and then to translate that vision into reality."

- Warren Bennis

Introduction

There are so many leadership concepts out there. Some good, some great and some that just shouldn't be out there at all! Overall though, there's some pretty good stuff to be had from friends, mentors and from trawling the internet on how to be a more effective leader. When it comes down to it, you need to try what you can and keep what works for you. We're all different and so are the people we lead.

At times, even the stuff you know usually works won't work, so it's good to keep on learning and especially let other people make the mistakes. So what's new in this book? Well, my experience has shown me that books like this can hold a few great little nuggets and I promise this will be no exception. As you read through this book or take a look at the material as a reference guide, you will come across some principles you may have heard of and others that may be new to you. As with all reading, it's best to keep an open mind and be ready for those moments where that flash of inspiration comes to you and is applicable to you and your role right now.

You may have read books before and felt okay about what you've read. You may have even been moved to action and I hope at times, while reading this work that you will feel inspired to make changes and to act in the areas that are relevant for you right now.

You may even return to the book and find new pieces of information that you didn't notice before because your circumstances may be different. You may be struggling with a difficult staff member this week and the next you may be struggling to keep your staff on track with an imminent change. So even if you read this book all the way through in one go don't think that you're done, as parts of it will mean more at different times. And certainly don't ever think you've learned all there is to know about leadership because you won't. Situations change, people change and so do all of the factors surrounding them - work, life and all that makes up your world in each successive moment.

What is a team?

There are a number of definitions you could attribute to a team. Teams differ from other types of groups in that they are focused on a achieving a common purpose or goal.

"A team is a small number of people with complementary skills who are committed to a common purpose, performance goals, and approach for which they are mutually accountable."

- (Katzenbach, J.R. & Smith, D.K. (1993). *The Wisdom of Teams: Creating the High-performance Organization.* Boston: Harvard Business School)

Take a look at your team at the moment. Does it sound like the definition above? Let's take a look at some of these components:

Small number of people: Your team may be made up of two or 22 people. The number is undefined. If you are leading a team of 100, then you will have some struggles if you intend to lead them all individually. You should break them up into smaller groups led by leaders who report to you. What is the best practice for numbers in a team? Well, again, this is a debatable point and depends largely on the factors of their work and your responsibilities. Normally though, a range of six to 15 would be normal. Numbers greater than this will mean you will struggle to perform your leadership role effectively.

Complementary Skills: The reason your team should be made up of people with complementary skills is so you have a good spread of abilities that together will help achieve the goal or objective in mind. If everyone in the team has the same skill sets then there is unlikely to be any learning effect and you may achieve a limited number of results. For example, if your team skills are all ideas-based, you may come up with amazing ideas but nothing will come to fruition. You need someone who can take the ideas to the next stage and someone else who can implement them, someone else to keep track or schedules etc.

Committed to a common purpose: There are two parts to this component. Firstly, the word committed indicates that the people in the team should have this as their focus. They need to believe in the cause or the outcome you're trying to reach. If people are idling their way through, you will take longer to achieve a less satisfactory result. The common purpose part is about having a shared vision. It's your job as the leader to create this shared vision and help the team know what it is and keep their eyes on the goal.

Mutually accountable: Accountability is a driving motivator. If someone knows that they are the one responsible for achieving an outcome and that the buck stops with them, they are more likely to be engaged. Share the accountability with the team. Help them see that together you are all accountable and together you will share in the credit, the benefits and the results.

"It's surprising how much you can accomplish, if you don't care who gets the credit."

- Abraham Lincoln

Leadership and management

There have been many arguments about the differences between leadership and management. Some people believe they are synonymous and others argue about the subtle differences. For me, the distinction is simple:

Leaders lead people and managers manage tasks.

No one wants to be managed or supervised. Those terms have the connotation that someone isn't capable of working without someone being there to ensure they work properly. People want to be inspired and motivated to work and perform well.

Leadership is about the passion, the motivation and desire to get something done. As a leader you will be wearing both the leader's hat and the manager's hat. It's part of your role to figure out which hat to wear on which occasion. There's no doubt that sometimes you will need to make sure processes are followed, work is completed and reports are done (managerial tasks) and there are other times when you will be helping your team get behind the vision, discover their values and need to draw on their strengths (leadership).

Consider even how your words are used in both speech and in writing and you will be able to identify whether they are leadership words or managerial words. You may notice the difference in the response you receive too. Consider your email subject lines for example. Is the subject a phrase that focuses on the task or on the passion to complete the task?

The brain

We know that the brain is made of two halves, one of which focuses on the logical, functional aspects (the left side) and the other which focuses on the creative and imaginative side (the right side). It's the latter which you can tap into regarding inspiring through your leadership skills.

Stephen Covey refers to a group working in the forest. The leader is the one who is with the team helping them to cut down the trees. He is there to help them make the correct swing with the axe, ensuring that the head is sharp and that they are working well together. The manager is in a tower making sure they are cutting down the right forest. In this simple illustration, you can see that the leader is with the people. They are not removed, poring over some report sending instructions by memo. A leader is with the team observing, motivating, correcting where necessary and ensuring the right effort is exerted and the job completed.

When the ancient Greeks of Platea marched in unison in battle it was the job of the Paraclete at the end of the line to motivate the group as they marched forward. He held a long spear and walked with the line shouting words of encouragement. His role was to keep the troops from running away and he would offer statements of hope as they marched, often to certain death. The word Paraclete itself means 'Hope is near'. As a leader, you should be there to offer hope and help the team see that their goals are achievable, practical and that you'll help them achieve them.

Take a moment and write down a few leaders you admire. You could consider current or former heads of countries - like Winston Churchill, leaders in their fields of expertise past or present like Steve Jobs or those you may know personally. What is it you admire about them? What character traits do they exhibit? Are there some collective traits which you would like to emulate?

Think about yourself. What are some of the characteristics about you that make you a good leader? Are there areas for improvement?

> **Tip:** Leaders lead people and managers manage tasks.

"The boss drives people; the leader coaches them. The boss depends on authority; the leader on good will. The boss inspires fear; the leader inspires enthusiasm. The boss says "I"; the leader says "WE". The boss fixes the blame for the breakdown; the leader fixes the breakdown. The boss says, "GO"; the leader says "LET'S GO!" "

- H. Gordon Selfridge

Are you a good leader?

Having staff and being a leader can be both rewarding and frustrating. If you find it rewarding you are either doing some things right or are just darn lucky. If you find it frustrating, you may just be unlucky or you could benefit from the following tips on how to motivate your staff and be a manager that staff will want to work for. Although the following ideas are not an exhaustive list, they are some of the fundamentals that can help to make a good leader.

Acknowledge your staff

When a member of staff does a job well, make sure you notice it, and acknowledge her or him for it. Don't let the opportunity to praise a piece of good work go by. Be careful that you don't embarrass them as some people don't like public recognition and others do. Learn what type of praise each of your staff members prefer and treat them accordingly. Everyone likes a compliment and it can greatly improve motivation and morale to reinforce good behaviour by acknowledging it. If they stay a little late to finish something off, if they put some extra effort in or whatever it is, a simple thank you can be very effective.

Never, ever humiliate anyone on your team

If you are annoyed with someone on your team, or they have done something wrong, make sure you keep your cool, especially in public. If you humiliate someone, he or she will hold a grudge against you, and their work will suffer too. Always deal with difficult situations in private. If you have to give corrective feedback to someone, ensure it is directly with them. Don't try and do it in a group.

Create a culture where mistakes are okay

If you don't make mistakes, chances are you are not stretching yourself. If your staff members are allowed to feel that mistakes are part of reaching for new highs, rather than something to feel bad about, or ashamed of, then they will take more risks on your behalf. In some cases, mistakes just need to be avoided but if you expect your staff to think for themselves, try out new things and stretch themselves a bit – then they may sometimes fall short but at least they'll be trying. Help them understand that making a mistake may mean they need to fix it and making the same mistake repeatedly is not acceptable.

Remember personal details

Take time to get to know your staff, who they are, who and what is important in their lives, etc. Be interested in them as people, not just as workers. People will be more motivated to please you when they feel personally connected. Try to remember the small details. Listen to them. Ask them about their weekend, their plans etc. If they know you care there'll be no stopping them.

Don't hide behind your position

Be human and friendly with your staff – that way you will all be able to support and encourage each other when things are tough. It's okay if you don't agree with everything from the top. It's okay if you're struggling with things too. If you communicate well and share frustrations but show how you are trying to support management as well, they'll see you're human.

Be approachable

Allow your staff to feel that they can come and talk to you about sensitive issues, about inside – and outside – work difficulties, and that you will respect them, and not hold what they share against them. This means that you actually make time for them and not just say that you are there for them.

Admit your mistakes

If you get it wrong, say so. Managers don't have to be infallible! Your staff will respect you more if you are able to admit your mistakes, and then set about sorting out a solution. An honest, no excuses apology or admission of a mistake is very powerful. If you cover everything up, they'll know and you'll lose their trust. If you can show that it's okay to take responsibility and how you fix it, then they will respect you for it.

Listen in such a way that your employees will talk to you

Often people feel afraid of, or intimidated by, management. Make sure you show people that you are willing to listen to what they have to say, that they are important and worthy of your time.

Be clear in your requests

It is your responsibility to ensure that people understand your requests – so communicate clearly, and ask if people have understood what you are asking for. Many hours of wasted work and effort can be spent because a leader hasn't been clear in their requests. Confirm their understanding so you know they are going to do what you want done. See the section later on setting clear expectations for more details on this.

Treat everyone respectfully and courteously at all times

Particularly when there is a problem! Everyone who works for you is a valuable human being who deserves respect. A manager is only as good as how she or he treats the people on her or his team.

Being a good manager takes effort and consistency.

> **Tip:**   Don't forget the little things. Remember personal details, admit your mistakes, share the credit.

"Leadership is the art of getting someone else to do something you want done because he wants to do it."

- Dwight D. Eisenhower

What do I focus on as a leader of a team?

There are many areas to focus on and sometimes this means that you will ironically lose focus. Consider what will be your critical success factors – those things you will be measured on by your superiors. These measures then will lead into critical activities.

Consider the coach of a basketball team. It's obvious they are watching both the scoreboard and the game. If they just watched the scoreboard they may miss vital information about how the game is being played. The team may be performing brilliantly and being just unlucky and yet the coach could change everything in the hope that the change could change the score.

Conversely, if the coach just watched the game, he may miss the fact that time is ticking away or that they need a change of tactic to get a different result.

As a leader of a team, you can't just rely on statistics and data. Neither can you ignore those facts. You need to look at the statistics and observe the performance. They go together and seeing them both in perspective and hand in hand puts you in a better place to make decisions.

Critical activities

No matter what your role is, there will be core activities that you must focus on that will provide you with the results you need to achieve. If you're not sure what those activities are, make a list of the things you feel you need to accomplish in a month. For each of those activities on the list, link through to a key measure or KPI (key performance indicator) that you are measured on in your role. Those activities that lead directly to a KPI or key measure that you have responsibility for are the critical activities you must do. Don't discount areas though that you find difficult to link through to the measures. For example, coaching your team may not be a direct measure you are given as a KPI but if you don't coach them then their performance is likely to drop off or not improve. Believe the fact that whatever your team are measured on, that's where their focus will be so long as there are consequences in place for poor or non-performance.

Four areas you can focus on as a leader to help your team achieve and perform well, namely: Give direction, coach, monitor and recognise.

Give direction

This means that you are talking to your team regularly and frequently about what is happening, targets, goals, performance and about improvements that can be made. People want to be kept informed and clear, open communication falls under this vital component of a leader's responsibility. Tell people what's going on and help them have no doubt as to what they need to do and how it fits in the bigger picture.

Coach

Coaching is an essential component of leading and allows you to reinforce desired behaviours and embed them as normal into the team. Remember that good coaches aren't just watching the scoreboard – they watch the game as well. Some days the scoreboard just won't reflect the effort and the performance. You need to watch both! This means that you need to observe your team members in action and provide effective feedback on the behaviours you see. Coaching can be rewarding for both you and your team members. Learn good coaching skills as it will have the biggest impact on your team.

Monitor

You need to be able to track the progress of your team. Be careful here though and monitor only those areas that are really important. Remember that what we measure we focus on. Review what you're measuring regularly. If you don't know why you are measuring something it's probably not worth measuring. If it's not having an impact on the business or the team, why bother? When performance is measured, performance increases. When it's reported on, the rate of improvement actually accelerates, so make sure you report back on those measures.

Recognise

People like to receive recognition. It doesn't matter if it's their job they're performing, reinforce the performance by recognising it. Make sure though that however you choose to recognise someone, it's done in the form desired by the recipient. Use recognition early when you are trying to instil new behaviours as it will encourage the continuation of those behaviours. Ensure that you are sincere and avoid overdoing it as it will become diluted. Consider recognition when people consistently perform at a high standard, when they exceed your expectations, go above and beyond, or when you feel they need a bit more motivation.

The Pygmalion Effect

The Pygmalion Effect was described in the Harvard Business review in 1988 by J. Sterling Livingston as the following: "The way managers treat their subordinates is subtly influenced by what they expect of them". Every leader has expectations of the people who report to him or her. These expectations are communicated either consciously or unconsciously and people will pick up on them. People will then perform in ways that are consistent with the expectations they have picked up from their supervisor.

It's really a self-fulfilling prophecy then for people as they start to act the way you, as their leader, expect them to act. This can be very positive as staff members begin to excel in response to their leader's message that they are capable of success and are indeed capable of succeeding. A leader can however get the opposite effect by not treating all employees the same or by failing to praise someone where it is due.

A leader can extend the effect when they hold positive expectations of their staff. Just holding those positive expectations means they will naturally help improve the self-esteem of their people and individuals in turn believe in themselves and their performance rises to meet their own expectations.

Tip: A good coach or leader watches both the scoreboard and the game. One of the two is not enough to understand what exactly is going on.

"Leadership has a harder job to do than just choose sides. It must bring sides together."

- Jesse Jackson

Goal setting

Setting goals is a great way to help your team see that they are achieving and it helps to get the work done. You may already have a set number of KPIs (Key performance indicators). These are measures that are in place to help management see that things are on the right track and that the critical activities are being focused on.

One of the errors some leaders make is to focus on the wrong stuff. They may be busy alright but in the wrong areas or in doing things that don't really matter that much or that don't have a massive impact on the team or the business. Take reports for example. They're necessary but some people spend most of their time wrapped up in doing administration rather than leading the people. A leader's job is to be with the team and help them to achieve. You can't do that effectively from behind a desk.

Some leaders say they know what's going on because they can see their team from where they're sitting. I challenge you to know what is actually going on in those conversations with customers from your desk. You need to watch, observe, listen and engage with you team to fully understand what is happening. If you lead a team of sales people who are out on the road, you can't possibly know what is going on unless you spend time with them. Go with them to occasional meetings and find out how they operate.

So, in order to help stretch your team members, help them to set meaningful and achievable goals. Consider using the SMART goal method:

- Specific
- Measurable
- Agreed
- Realistic
- Time-bound.

Be specific in what it is you want them to achieve. You can't say for example that you want them to improve their performance. It just isn't specific and you will then be in an argument about what improvement looks like. So when you set goals and want to be specific, describe what it is you want them to achieve.

In fact guide them to come up with the goal where possible. If they decide upon it, they will be more likely to want to achieve it. You may ask, "How many calls do you think you can make this week?" This gives them the opportunity to come up with the number. Now if it's too low, you may need to coach them a bit around being realistic, stretching, being sensible etc but help them come up with it. Once you have the goal, just make sure it is specific and then measurable. Will you be able to actually measure that they have achieved it when it is complete.

Do not impose goals on your team. If they don't own the goal, they will feel much less inclined to go for it. This is the 'agreed' part of the acronym.

Goals should be realistic and achievable. There's no point having a goal so high that it's impossible. Some people think that if you set goals really high they may still get somewhere well but if they never achieve goals, they will always be looked on as out of reach and never believe they will get there.

Finally ensure that there is a timescale involved. People need to know when the deadline is. Without a timeframe, a goal will remain open-ended forever.

The SMART goal provides some boundaries for people to stay inside of. People need boundaries but they don't want rules to be so rigid that there is no room for individuality or interpretation.

When you have your goals set with your team, let them know what the follow up plan is. Let them know when and how they will need to report back to you. If there is no accountability at the end, or a goal, then they may never achieve it and you may never know either way.

No accountability means people will see no value in the goal. Hold people accountable and give them all the support they need to get it accomplished. Don't strangle them with leadership though. Give them space. In fact, talk to them about how they would like you involved. Do they want regular catch ups or not. Do they want you to comment on how they are doing? These things are personal preferences. You may need to vary things up for different people.

You could consider using the GROW model which is another coaching technique. The GROW model or technique was developed in the UK and used extensively in the 1980s and 1990s.

The four stages are:

- Goal
- Reality
- Options / Obstacles
- Way forward.

The Goal is the end point - where you need to be at the end. This is why it needs to be SMART so there is no ambiguity about what is to be achieved, by when.

The Reality is the gap between the current situation and where the goal is. This is best looked at as a self-assessment from the team member. This needs to be real and clear. You may need to help them understand exactly what the gap is. You may like to help set a number of steps in place to be achieved on the way to the goal. It's easier to achieve small steps than one huge one.

Options can then be discussed to look at ways to overcome any obstacles. Discuss and offer options that could be considered. This is a great place to ask powerful questions like, "What do you think you will need to change to actually achieve this goal?"

The Way Forward is to decide upon the next steps, identify what support is needed and include review dates and possibilities. Ensure you end positively.

Tip: Ensure that each goal you set comes with accountability. Work on having your team member set the goal. Your job is to guide them in ensuring it is realistic.

"People ask the difference between a leader and a boss... The leader works in the open and the boss in covert. The leader leads and the boss drives."

- Theodore Roosevelt

Motivating your staff

Admit it, some days motivating your staff is like pushing rope! It's that silver bullet of management – keeping your staff motivated on a sustained basis. There are short term fixes like buying them ice creams on a hot day or longer term tricks like reward and recognition schemes. We've all seen the survey results about what motivates people to come to work but what gets them to do their work once they get there? The three big motivators can summed up as:

- The Need to Achieve
- The Craving to Contribute
- The Burn to Learn.

If you're stuck for motivational ideas – try to link back to one of these as you won't go wrong. Here are some great ways here to keep your staff motivated:

Goal setting

Do you and your staff have a clear idea of what it is you need to achieve, when you need to achieve it and how? Do you have one goal for the company or do individuals have their individual goals to meet to help achieve the company goals? Is the goal's progress fed back to the team on a regular and constructive basis? Do they feel like they are an integral part of the organisation? People want to feel like they are contributing and that their work is meaningful. Let them know how their efforts impact the big picture.

Sense of achievement / positive reinforcement

Catch people doing things right instead of always waiting for them to make a mistake. A simple but powerful statement such as "You did a great job today" or "Thanks for that" go a long way and cost nothing. Everyone likes personal recognition. Do not engage in empty praise. Always make it meaningful.

Reachable / attainable targets

Are targets set at a realistic and achievable level – high enough to stretch staff to find levels within themselves but not too high or too distant for people to give up? If targets are too easy, staff will not stretch themselves. Find the balance and watch the difference.

External versus internal stimuli

What is the balance between staff self-motivation and the drive to get things done and the need to constantly push or punish staff into doing the same things? External motivation is short lived, whereas internal motivation remains – even when you are not there. Do you know, I mean really know, what motivates your staff? If not, then take time to find out - it will pay dividends in the long term.

Honesty

Do not mislead or lie to your staff. People react better to direct honesty. Even if it is a hard call, make it, they will appreciate your honesty. If you make a mistake, own up to it. Never criticise in public.

Support

Do they have the support they need? Do they get the mentoring and coaching they may require to help them when they need it?

Direction / Vision

Does your team have crystal clear vision of where the company is going and why? Vision statements on the walls are not enough. Your company vision needs to be constantly in focus – talked about, planned, measured and refocused. If people buy into your vision for themselves, the company will become an exciting place to work.

For people to be able to do something well, they need to have three things:

1. Knowledge of what to do
2. Skills for performing the task
3. A desire to do it.

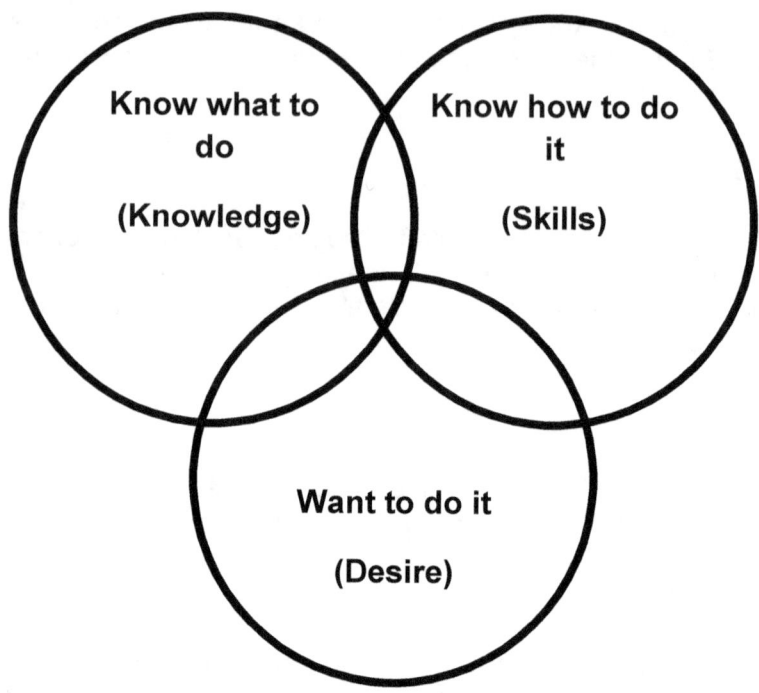

It's no good just having one or two of those things – all three are needed in order to get the best result.

When you're motivated to do something, you will be much more likely to accomplish it faster and more efficiently than when you're not. Motivation is our driving force. We are all motivated by different things and when we find ourselves 'in flow' where the time just whizzes by, we know that we are motivated in doing what we are doing.

Unless the person being coached wants to change or listen to you, it's unlikely that anything will change at all. The person needs to have the desire to change. People try all sorts of methods to motivate staff members, and coaching is no different. What we really want is for the coachee to want to change their behaviour or to want to do what it is we are recommending. If we take the various motivation options, we could put them into a simple matrix:

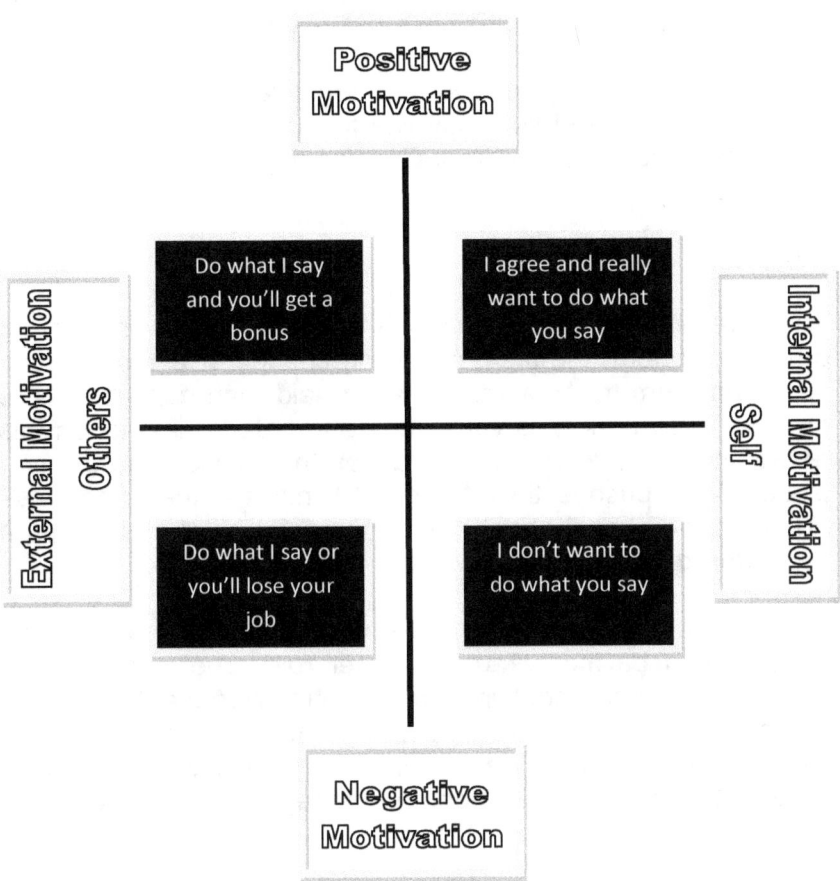

Basically, unless the person wants to change or do what's required, the likelihood is that they won't! Using negative motivation (for example - do it or you're fired!) may only gain a short term positive response. Like any external motivation, once the external motivation has gone, so has the desire. Even with positive motivation – if it's externally pushed (for example - do it and you'll get a prize) will mean that when the prize is no longer there, the desire has gone too. You'll have to keep providing prizes to keep up the motivation and the chances are you'll have to start increasing the perceived value of the prizes to keep their interest. Oh, and by the way, their salary is not considered enough of a prize in most cases.

This motivation using positive and negative consequences is a fascinating topic and you may like to research a bit more. Try searching articles on 'Operant Conditioning' if you would like to know more.

'Why' not 'what'

The real winner for motivation is to help create an internal desire to perform the task, make the change or act in the way you want them to. Now that's easier said than done but there are some key principles you can use in order to impact on this result. Firstly, understand what drives the individual in the first place. What pushes their buttons? What are their interests? The more you know about them, the easier it will be to tie in a motivator to their role or task.

As an example, one person – we'll call her Mary - was struggling to be motivated to do her role. She worked for a government department in a call centre. Her great love was opera singing. How on earth was the manager going to find a link to help motivate her to improve her interactions with callers? During the discussion, the manager started to focus on the 'WHY' rather than the 'WHAT'.

So often we spend our energies talking about what people like to do and what motivates rather than why we like to do it or why it motivates them. During this discussion, Mary explained that she loved the way she made people feel after performing opera. They felt better somehow, lifted and happier. Once the manager got this information, she was able to help Mary see that by doing her job well, she could also make people feel better, lifted and happier by dealing with their queries and helping them resolve any issues. That was it! That was all Mary needed to get going and perform. She had discovered a link between what motivated her and her job.

Getting this right will help you get buy-in from the individual. Buy-in means that you see the benefits and want to proceed with it 100%. It's more than supporting the idea and certainly more than accepting it. We all accept the price of petrol – because we pay it – but I don't think we all have buy-in for the price it is set at. We're not eagerly queuing up to fill our tanks the minute we see the needle dip just below full – we're more likely to drive to the near-limit of the tank before we grudgingly go to the petrol pumps. Support for something means that we will tell people it's a good idea. We see some benefits. We might pay a contribution to a cause because we support it but we might not be up at 4am to join in the protest march or do without the new TV and donate all the money.

It's not until we really get behind something – live and breathe it, see that it's the only way and drive ourselves there without the need for someone else - that we have buy-in. When the manager has left for the day, we continue on as normal because we are internally motivated to do so. We are not relying on the manager watching us to perform at our best.

Tip: Remember that everyone wants to achieve, contribute and learn – these are the three basic motivators.

"No man will make a great leader who wants to do it all himself, or to get all the credit for doing it."

- Andrew Carnegie

Getting your team to work better together

I think most leaders would like their teams to work together better at some point. Perhaps the team is new or the dynamics just aren't sitting right or maybe the team has never really functioned as well as it could. I'd like to suggest some ways that your team could understand each other better and work together more effectively.

Communication

Fundamentally the simplest area to look at is how the team is communicating. Having open and honest communication can take away the 'indirect language' that causes confusion and assumptions. As the leader, you should lead by example and ensure that what you say is clear and to the point. Encourage the type of communication with each other in the team to be the same. One simple test is to ask team members to make sure 'an exchange of understanding' has taken place. This means clarifying and checking understanding. It's not enough to say: "I sent you an email" or: "I told you about that". It's important to check that people both receive and understand the communication.

Share preferences

Have the team members get in the habit of sharing their preferred way of dealing with work things. For example, if someone prefers to have time to think about a topic rather than be expected to share opinions on it at short notice encourage them to declare that preference. Some people get annoyed when people don't speak up at meetings when it just may be the person's preference to think things through. If people hate it when agendas aren't adhered to, learn to understand that preference. When team members are sensitive to other's preferences, they understand them and their point of view much better. Consider your team's preferences in organisational work habits, meetings, processes and communication areas especially. You could take five minutes at each team meeting to take turns for everyone to share a preference or two. These preferences can be explored well using the Team Management Index (TMP Profile).

Express thanks & celebrate successes

Take time out to thank, enjoy and celebrate when things have gone well. Cultivate a culture of appreciation - even if it's for people doing their job. When an achievement is made which is out of the ordinary, take time to celebrate the achievement. If people feel appreciated, they are likely to respond better when you need them to push a bit further or stay a bit later. Showing appreciation, giving compliments and rewards all help to motivate people.

Accountability

Establish a culture of accountability. If someone is not pulling their weight, you need to address it. Team members that work hard see when others aren't putting in the same effort. You need to show to the whole team that fairness is a principle you want to adopt. You can build trust faster in a team when you hold each team member accountable for their efforts and results. Consider consequences for non-performance or below par effort. Positive consequences for good performance will include areas in point 3 above.

Share responsibility

Help develop the team by sharing responsibility. Delegate some tasks to help develop skills. Challenge the team so they are given opportunities to grow and stretch. This means they may make mistakes - make sure that's okay and help them to learn and recover from them. If you don't allow mistakes people won't want to try new things because they'll be too afraid to. Remember that if you are looking for a promotion at some point, you want to have someone prepared to take over your role otherwise you may not get the chance.

Tip: Work on having clear, transparent communication. Ensure that there is an exchange of understanding.

"Leadership is an action, not a position."

- Donald H. McGannon

Effective coaching

Coaching is about carrying, transporting or moving somebody from one state or place to another. It is really about helping people resolve their own issues and discover their own potential. Coaching is not about lecturing or telling people what to do or solving all their problems. Although you may need to instruct or direct from time to time, the major role of a coach is to help the coachee find the solution themselves. This method of self-discovery is a fundamental leadership skill and can make all the difference.

If you believe you are coaching someone else because you are more capable than the other person, you are looking at coaching incorrectly. In many cases, the person being coached will know more about the systems, processes, products, services and even customers than you will. It's not about being the hero or the rescuer. It's not about looking smart or showing that you know everything. It's about helping people know how to come to solutions on their own, develop strategies for a better way of thinking and facilitating issues so they have total ownership.

You can do all this by developing your own questioning, listening and paraphrasing skills. As a coach, you need to develop skills in 'drawing' information out of people.

The aim of good coaching is to facilitate a discussion. This means that your task is to 'draw out' information from the person you are coaching. It's about helping them discover themselves the answers and solutions. Self-discovery is a term to be aware of as a leader. Use it to ensure you are not just lecturing or telling people what to do.

Reinforcing feedback

There are two basic types of coaching or giving feedback.

The first is Reinforcing feedback. This is when you are feeding back to the individual that what they have done or doing is the right thing. It helps if this is done as soon as possible after the behaviour is demonstrated. The impact is always greatest as soon after as possible. The Time / Impact curve demonstrates this:

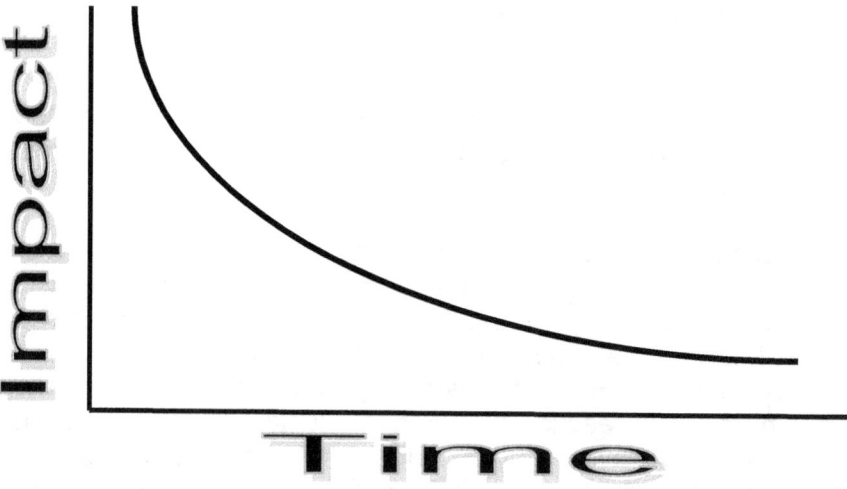

The longer you leave something, the less the impact has on the individual.

In reinforcing feedback, you would describe what has been done and discuss the impact it has had. For example, if a staff member resolved a query then explained to the customer that to save time on their next query they could register their query on the website and someone would call them back at a convenient time for them and the leader wanted to coach on that, the leader could say,

> *"When you offered that service to the customer about registering future queries that way, you really added some great value that they weren't expecting. It shows you understand the future needs of the customer extremely well. You didn't have to say it but you did and that customer has a better view of our company as a result. Great work. Keep it up."*

The staff member would feel acknowledged, reassured for giving the information and great about what they did as well as having the reasons reinforced by their leader. Everyone wins.

Corrective feedback

The other type of feedback is corrective feedback. This is best done right before the person has an opportunity to use it. This means that it is often wasted at the end of the day for example as they will just be reflecting on the feedback and not on the impact it could have.

This type of feedback is well done if you are coaching someone live in a setting where you are taking calls together, making sales visits or in the work environment live. For example, if you wanted a staff member to try out a new technique to pause after asking for a sale, you could say,

> "Okay, on this next call, after you have asked them for the business, just pause and don't say

anything until they speak next. Let them speak first okay?"

Once the staff member tries it out and sees the effect, they'll have additional confidence in what you've told them and keep using it. If you said it a week earlier, there's little chance they will remember to do it and therefore not reap any associated benefits.

Coaching the right way

In order to coach the right way, we need to understand what the wrong way is. Let's face it, we have all had some experience where coaching hasn't been very effective. In fact, I have had organisations say to me that they have regular coaching but nothing changes. Their leaders coach each month, people commit and then hold the same conversations the next month again with no change. This is a classic example of coaching on activators in order to change behaviours.

Activators are those items that cause us to do something. In themselves they have some motivation behind them. For example, an activator we all have is hunger. This activator leads us to do a certain behaviour which is to feed ourselves. This behaviour leads to a consequence which is that we become full (or put on weight)!

So, there are three components in this process:

The activator is the driver of the behaviour.

The behaviour is what is done.

The consequence is the result.

Coaching that is not done well is coaching that is focused on the activator. This is coaching that focuses on words like, "do more, do better, faster, increase, slow down, improve" etc. people then under pressure or wishing to please say, "Okay". Leaders then feel they have a commitment and are surprised that the behaviour hasn't changed. They then coach more and say the same stuff but louder, bolder etc.

However, if the consequence is changed, the behaviour is much more likely to be altered. Think about these two examples:

1. If you were thirsty (activator) and you put $2 in a drinks machine (behaviour) you would expect a drink (consequence). However, if the drink did not come out as a result, you are not likely to keep putting $2 in the machine. The consequence is dramatically different that it has changed your behaviour. You are more likely to kick the machine or call someone up about it rather than keep putting money in.

2. If the room got dark as a result of the sun going down (activator) and you turned the light switch on (behaviour) you would expect the light to come on (consequence). However, if the light did not work, you would not keep turning the light switch on (apart from that frantic on/off pressing until you realised it won't work). You would source an alternative light source like a torch.

So, you can see that with these two examples, the change in the consequence made a huge impact on the actual behaviour exhibited.

Now think about your people and their roles. What example can you start with where you want behaviour to change? What is the activator and the normal consequence? What can you change the consequence to be in order for the behaviour to change?

Some coaching is done to tick a box. I.e. a leader feels they must coach so they do (not very well) and tick the coaching box. Coaching is not a passive action; it needs to be engaging, thought through and personal to the individual. You cannot hope to coach everybody the same way. People in your team will have preferences and needs that vary.

You can find many more tips on coaching and effective feedback in one of my other books entitled, "Coaching and feedback made easy", details of which are at the end of this book.

Tip: Focus on changing the consequence to successfully change the behaviour.

"The challenge of leadership is to be strong, but not rude; be kind, but not weak; be bold, but not bully; be thoughtful, but not lazy; be humble, but not timid; be proud, but not arrogant; have humor, but without folly."

- Jim Rohn

Dealing with conflict

As a leader, managing conflict is part of your role. It comes with the territory and you can use conflict that exists as a positive in your team. Don't be afraid of conflict. In basic terms, conflict can be a difference of opinion. It's healthy and helps to innovate and create ideas. Avoidance of conflict is often the topic that people discuss. A lot of people would rather avoid conflict than deal with it because they only see the negative effects.

Some people don't stand up for their beliefs or their opinions and this only serves to have a group of people that say 'yes' to their leader or others and then the opportunity for improvement, tweaking, discussion and change is often lost. It's often the case that when you have a group that feels like they can't offer opinions or agree on what to do but complain about the decision later on and then you have a dissention issue which is often harder to fix. Conflict handled well means people don't get hurt and don't take things personally. It's your role to ensure that you don't harm these relationships.

Set a clear expectation that it is okay to have a differing opinion and that a healthy debate can lead to a more defined and agreed outcome. Encourage others to speak up and express their opinion. Help them see the benefits of this. When it's time to agree or move forward with a decision then you can sum up, acknowledge the opinions and share the reasons for any decision that's been arrived at. Thank those who have offered opinions. Don't shoot people down in public for sharing ideas. Examine your own behaviours and see if you encourage opinions or somehow shut them down instead.

It's always useful to have others support their opinions with facts or data. This will help you in resolving conflicts between people if you can get them to recognise that the facts are the starting point. Supporting information is a great way to illuminate a problem. Get used to asking a question like, "What are the reasons for you coming to that conclusion?"

When encouraging opinions in your team, help the team understand that personal attacks are not tolerated. If people feel that there is equality, fairness and safety in expressing thoughts and opinions, you will get much more impact and variety as well as happier staff. You can train your staff in conflict handling and problem solving skills.

Understand the type of conflict

Conflict situations can be of various types and include:

- Functional conflict: This is a disagreement with plans, policies or procedures

- Role-based conflict: This is a disagreement over the role someone is in or asked to perform

- Emotional conflict: This type of conflict involves basic feelings of anger, frustration, fear, jealousy etc.

It's important to identify the type of conflict before trying to sort it out. For example, if you try to fix someone's emotions that are actually being caused by a functional conflict, the resolution will be short lived. You will need to correct the functional issue first. Make sure that whatever you come up with as a solution that doesn't have any road blocks to prevent it being successful.

Methods of dealing with conflict in your team

Don't meet with antagonists separately. Allowing each person to individually share their views will only strengthen and polarise each position. They will see it as imperative that you understand their position and side with them. Meet with them together. Allow them to summarise and briefly share their views without the other party interrupting. If there are personal attacks, intervene.

Consider your role as a facilitator. Practice asking questions of those in the conflict that make them think about their position such as:

"What are the reasons for you proposing that?"

"Can we find a way to do this without criticizing each other personally?"

"What could you do to change?"

"What can you do more of, less of, start doing?"

"What impact do you think your behaviour has on the rest of the team?"

"What will you do next time this happens?"

"Can you explain that to me in a different way?"

"If we can't' agree, what will the consequences be?"

Come up with some questions of your own that help the people involved see that you want to help and that you expect them to come up with a solution that will work. It's not about asking them to shake hands and make up; it's about coming to an understanding on both sides and seeing the middle ground - a win-win if you like.

You can ask them to describe specific actions they would like the other to take with reasons for requesting those actions. For example, "I'd like Peter to give me the weekly data from the team by Thursday at 5pm so I can produce the report by Friday lunchtime." Help them commit to noticing that the other person has made a change, even if it is small. This is helping to acknowledge the effort of the other person.

Let them know that you will not choose sides and that you expect them to sort out the conflict as adults. If they refuse, explain that you will need to take it further which could lead to disciplinary action (always check with your HR representative first). Be sure that you always follow official processes.

Reassure them that you have every confidence in their ability to resolve the issue. Record the agreements and always set a time to review.

Be prepared to say no. Set some boundaries. Don't let people get away with saying things that are just not fair or are out of line and always ensure there are no personal attacks. If one person is out on their own with an opinion, you can ask if anyone else feels the same way. If they don't then maybe you have a strong case for moving on claiming that as they are the only ones with a diverse view. Thank them for it and move on.

Some conflict situations will highlight that someone is potentially in the wrong role and you may need to rethink positions, roles, responsibilities and relationships. Remember the old adage, if you can't change the people, change the people. If people just won't improve, alter their behaviours or be willing to compromise, then maybe it's time to move them out.

In any conflict situation, you must deal with it. You can't hope that it goes away. Deal with it quickly. Remind people about team charters, company objectives, the company's vision and mission – anything that will help those involved see that their behaviour is not in line with established procedures or policy.

> **Tip:** In conflict, you don't come up with the solution, you help the antagonists arrive at a win-win position and leave with a shared understanding.

"He who has never learned to obey cannot be a good commander."

- Aristotle

Dealing with difficult behaviours

When you have team members reporting to you, it's natural for some to exhibit difficult behaviours. Basically any behaviour that is causing you concern or impacting negatively on the rest of the team or the business could be termed as difficult. One of the key things for you to remember and to be aware of is to keep calm, stay in control and resolve the issue.

Difficult behaviours from staff are like difficult behaviours from customers. Most of the problem lies with the emotion rather than the issue or what's causing the behaviour. Unlike coaching, you may need to have a focus on the activator rather than the consequence as you will need to remove or resolve the activator first.

People naturally have a defence mechanism built into them commonly known as the 'fight or flight' response. It's that moment when you make a split decision to either fight and make a stand or run away to fight another day. Although our process time to think things through may have provided us with a different (and sometimes better) response, our immediate 'under pressure' response can be quite out of character and even damaging.

This response is caused by what's known as the amygdala hijack which is a term attributed to Daniel Goleman in his 1996 book *"Emotional Intelligence: Why It Can Matter More Than IQ"*. In the book, the term is used to describe emotional responses from people that are out of measure with the actual threat because it has triggered a much more significant emotional threat. In other words, the emotional reaction to what is in front of you has triggered something of greater emotional importance. Often we hear of people 'over reacting' and that is often due to their emotional understanding of a particular event being greater than our own.

The main types of responses can be put into three categories: fight, flight or freeze. When coaching someone and especially while giving feedback, people already put themselves in a higher emotional state. The things spoken about hit personal registers and put people under pressure so you can often come up against the following:

Fight response

People tend to get angry, argumentative, stop listening, are stubborn or even sarcastic. When experiencing this response, we might say something like:

"Don't speak to me like that!" or

"If you don't calm down I'll terminate the call."

Flight response

People here tend to want to avoid conflict, blame someone else, blame a system fault, or pass the buck in general. When experiencing this response, we might say:

"One of the others must have told you that."

"It's not my problem."

"Let me put you on to my manager"

Freeze response

Here's where your mind goes blank, you can't think of anything to say or you feel embarrassed.

The thing about the amygdala hijack is that it's automatic but we can control it. While our brain (cortex) is accessing its records for an appropriate response, the amygdale also receives the information and offers a shortcut immediate threat response and blocks off the 'slow thinking'. Our response to a situation will affect the outcome. If we think of the outcome in these terms: Outcome = Event + Response or written the other way: Event (E) = my response to the event, (R) = the outcome, then we know that:

> E – things that will happen
>
> R – how I choose to respond to it
>
> O – will determine the outcome or result.

As an example: If a staff member calls me names (E) and I get offended and shout back at them (R), then the outcome (O) is going to be conflict between us.

But...

If a staff member calls me names (E) and I ignore the name calling, keep calm and stick to the facts (R), then the outcome is going to be a more logical and productive discussion between us (O).

So, how I manage my response or reaction to things and people can determine the end result I want to get. It all sounds straight forward and actually is. The simple four step process to remember in each case of potential conflict is:

1. Pause

2. Listen and acknowledge the response or the behaviour

3. Return to the facts

4. Focus on a solution.

Here are a few examples of what can happen and how using this approach can assist. Let's take it that you are giving someone feedback on getting to work late:

Event	Response
Staff member cries	1. PAUSE 2. The aim of this discussion is not to upset you... 3. We are here to talk about the fact that you have been getting to work late. 4. Tell me why this is happening?
Staff member is aggressive (e.g. says something like: you are such a bad manager)	1. PAUSE 2. This discussion is not about me... 3. We are here to talk about the fact that you have been getting to work late. 4. We need to agree how you are going to manage to get to work on time.
Staff member is defensive (e.g. why are you picking on me?)	1. PAUSE 2. I am not picking on you... 3. The fact is, you have got to work more than 10 minutes late on the last 3 days. 4. Tell me why this is happening?
Staff member blames (e.g. I'm not the only one in the team who is doing it)	1. PAUSE 2. If it is happening with others, you can know that I will address it with them. Or what happens in other managers departments is not my issue. In this department, I expect my staff to get to

	work on time.
	3, We are here to talk about your lateness, so...
	4. Tell me why this is happening?
Staff member is silent	1. PAUSE
	2. If you don't talk to me, we cannot work together to fix it...
	3. As I mentioned, you have been late the last 3 days.
	4. Why is that?

In each one of these examples, you can manage the response by:

1. Pausing (to manage the amygdala hijack)

2. Not taking things personally (reminding yourself that it was an attempt to divert your attention)

3. Sticking to the facts

4. Keeping the conversation moving forward to a solution.

Tip: Stick to the facts. If you move off the facts, you are likely to have differences of opinions and you will find it hard to make your point.

"A good objective of leadership is to help those who are doing poorly to do well and to help those who are doing well to do even better."

- Jim Rohn

Dealing with bad attitudes

Bad attitudes in the workplace are a pain. As a manager, you may find yourself complaining about them to others and wish they'd just go away but how much of it is down to you? Attitudes of staff members may deteriorate due to a number of reasons so to avoid them in the first place or help turn them round, have a look at the following.

Be Fair

Look at how you work with your staff. Are they paid fairly? Do you treat them well and avoid showing favouritism? Staff will quickly develop resentment when fairness is not apparent in the workplace.

Listen

Do you listen to your staff? Most people want to feel like they are contributing. Ask them for their opinions. At times, show that you are acting on their suggestions and they will feel more integrated and important.

Communicate

Let your staff know what is happening. Don't keep them in the dark. Tell them what's going on in the business; share the plans, the feedback from customers and upper management.

Thank

Let them know that you appreciate them. Small courtesies like 'Thank you' are often overlooked but can go a long way to build trust and improve morale. A little extra effort of showing appreciation on your part can help turn round or avoid the negative attitude of your staff.

Steps to turn around bad attitudes

What you can do to help turn round existing bad attitudes is to follow these steps:

1. Note instances where their attitude has had a negative impact on the work. Their attitude may have caused people to avoid them which may have delayed a process. This could have caused a customer to miss out on a communication all because one of the team has not felt they were able to approach the person with the bad attitude. Record these instances so you can establish some facts.

2. Meet with the person that has the attitude and present your findings to them. Ask them to share their perspective. Just talking about it may help to dispel some of the issue. Stick to the facts so it is more difficult for them to argue.

3. Agree on what should happen as a result. Ask them to suggest what they can do to alter the situation. Get them to commit and follow up.

What you want to be able to do is reduce the reasons for someone to have a bad attitude, then if it happens, don't hope it goes away – act quickly because if you don't do something about it, you may lose the members of staff that you want to keep!

Tip: Keep an eye on what you are doing to ensure that you are not contributing to the bad attitudes of your staff – inconsistency of managers is one of the worst contributors to bad attitudes in the workplace.

"Confidence is contagious. So is lack of confidence."

- Michael O'Brien

Courageous conversations

There will definitely be times when you need to hold a difficult or courageous conversation. This basically means that you have a situation that needs addressing. There are some things that just don't go away or get worse the longer you leave them. It's not just the natural consequences for leaving things, it's also the pressure that builds up in you personally and that can lead to stress and be a real problem for leaders.

Many people put off having difficult conversations. There are lots of reasons. It may be that we just fear the outcome. We don't want to hurt our relationship with the other person. Maybe we don't want to feel uncomfortable, deal with the emotions of the other person or perhaps we are just not sure what will happen so we avoid it.

It may be that we are just feeling uncomfortable about something. Perhaps we're angry at someone, we're avoiding someone or something, we may be embarrassed or ashamed of something or just worried about the consequences of the conversation.

There are so many benefits from having the difficult conversation such as:

- The behaviour you're addressing can cease from that moment
- You can clear the air
- You can get more commitment from your staff members
- You feel less stressed
- People will trust and respect you more.

So, how do you start? Well identify what it is that you're not 100% comfortable with – this is the dissatisfaction component of how we are feeling. We need to make sure what it is that's making us uncomfortable and make that the focus. Now identify what it is that we want or need to express to the other party. Imagine the worst outcome that could happen as a result of having the conversation and accept that possibility. Let go of the thing that is holding you back and remember it's okay to feel uncomfortable and focus on the fact that at least after the conversation you won't have those feelings of trepidation any more – they'll be gone because you will have addressed it.

When you address the person, you can explain to the person that you have some difficult feedback to share if you like. Brace them for what may be coming. You can even say that you feel uncomfortable about having to give the feedback. Avoid telling them that it's someone else who has brought it to your attention. You could even say that the situation demands that you give the feedback. Get to the point quickly and link the change you expect to a positive business impact and agree on an action.

Let's say you need to address a personal hygiene problem with another member of staff. So, you've identified that the issue does in fact exist and you need to address it with them. The bonus for you is that they may not be aware of the issue and might be very grateful to you for bringing it to their attention. That is the best outcome of the situation and does happen sometimes.

However, you have to get there first and it's always good to be direct and get to the point fast. You may say something to this person along the lines of:

> *"I need to discuss something with you that is awkward and uncomfortable for me. I do hope that I don't offend you. You have had a noticeable body odour lately and I wanted to bring it to your attention as most people wouldn't know this about themselves."*

I suggest you then follow up with something that you believe may be the reason or cause. For example, if you notice they wear the same clothes all week long, you can suggest that it may have something to do with that.

At this point you will know whether the person is embarrassed or goes on the offensive. You will notice that in the suggested wording above, you didn't mention that people had complained about them – that will only make things worse. You have stayed with the facts by saying they have a noticeable body odour. If they do take a stance and refuse to admit it, you can remain on the factual slant and tell them that they need to respect the workplace and come to work clean.

You may also point other potential causes such as the list above and ask them to have a think about what they can do. Get them to commit to some action and make sure you follow up. Give yourself a reward task to do after dealing with the situation – you deserve it!

For any difficult or courageous conversation, you may like to follow the simple DESCCO steps. These steps are another great way to give or discuss feedback and can be done in a one-sided conversation way or by asking the other person to fill in each gap. It really does help to encourage self-discovery.

Here are the steps:

Describe the behaviour

Express how you felt

Specify what you'd prefer

Consequences of the new action

Contract to act in the new way

Ok.

Firstly, if you wanted to give direct feedback to someone say for complaining about everything you ask them to do, you might use it like this:

> "Peter, when you complain about my direction, I feel like you don't respect me as the leader of this team, I'd prefer it if you don't agree with what I've asked that you wait until you have an opportunity when you can address me personally, tell me why you don't like what you've heard and offer me an alternative. That way, you won't be disrupting everybody else and potentially distracting them in their work flow and together we may find a better solution. So, can I expect you to do that next time you feel like complaining in the group? Okay."

So, you'll see in that short paragraph that we used all the steps of DESCCO in a simple flow:

Describe: "When you complain about my direction…"

Express: "I feel like you don't respect me as the leader of this team."

Specify: "I'd prefer it that if you don't agree with what I've asked, please wait until you have…"

Consequences: "That way, you won't be disrupting everybody else and potentially distracting them in their work flow …"

Contract: "So, can I expect you to do that next time…"

Ok: "Okay."

Each of the steps has an important element to play in helping people to alter their behaviour. Firstly, describing what they did helps the person know exactly what it is you're talking about. It's therefore much more useful if the feedback given is descriptive (i.e. factual). The expression component then personalises it and gives some meaning to the effect of their behaviour. Specifying another way of approaching it gives them an alternative and explaining the consequences (which could be good or bad) gives reasoning for the person to consider the new behaviour suggestion. The contract is a way of getting them to concur or show their understanding. The ending with 'Okay' is for them to agree.

In our example above, we have shown a direct 'telling' method of giving feedback. Of course, it can be even more powerful if you switch the 'telling' to 'asking' in each of the steps of the DESCCO process after the 'Describe' step. For example, "When you shouted across the office, what impact do you think that had on the rest of the team?" This way you will be able to uncover their understanding and thinking a lot sooner and potentially gain greater buy-in.

You may need to have a difficult conversation on the phone, or when someone calls in sick. Maybe someone is away and decides to text you or email you. You really need to pick up the phone and hold the conversation. A difficult conversation is just that – it's a conversation. It's not a series of emails or texts.

There are lots of techniques you can try. You can even use the phrase, "If you were me, what would you do?" It's a great phrase to turn the tables and help the individual see things from your perspective.

There are many benefits for holding these conversations. In one particular organisation where there were four Team Leaders, the team that had the lowest absenteeism was the team where the leader held these types of conversations. When a staff member was absent, they would telephone them and ask what help they needed. They didn't avoid the situation. The team responded with more effort and recognised their own need to be accountable.

One thing is for sure, the more you hold these conversations, the easier they become and your confidence increases.

> **Tip:** Always link the change you want to a positive impact it will have on the business. Help them see that by changing their behaviour, there will be a positive business impact.

"The best executive is the one who has sense enough to pick good men to do what he wants done, and self-restraint enough to keep from meddling with them while they do it."

- Theodore Roosevelt

Delegation

Some people use lots of excuses for not delegating. Usually, their reasoning has no actual basis of truth – they just think it does. You'll get a lot more accomplished if you don't assume the following statements are true and use them as excuses for not delegating:

- I don't have time to show them how to do it

- They are already busy

- They aren't properly qualified I'm the only person who knows how to do this

- I could do a better job myself

- I can't trust them to do it

- No one else is available to delegate to

- They did a dreadful job last time

- I like doing all this stuff

We often spend time assuming the worst of people. We think they don't want to do what we ask them or that they just won't be up to the task. Consider changing your approach. Remember the Pygmalion effect from earlier on in the book. If we treat people like they can't do something or don't want responsibility, that's how they'll turn out.

Think about you personally, don't you want extra responsibility? People want to achieve, contribute and learn. They get all of these things by doing other tasks. Some short term investment in their development will pay off in the long term.

What can you delegate?

The first thing to remember is not to delegate something that doesn't need doing. Why are you doing it in the first place? Just stop doing it.

Try to delegate the routine stuff, even if you would rather not. This could include photocopying, collecting information, entering data, preparation of reports etc.

Look to delegate things that aren't part of your core role or skill set. You can't be an expert at everything, so delegate out the stuff that takes you longer than other people.

If you think there's nothing you can delegate, what happens when you're on holiday or on sick leave or if you had to take an extended leave of absence – is everything going to pile up for you? The more you have the ability to delegate, the more you can enjoy a day or more away from the business. If there's absolutely something you can't delegate, then okay but try to keep that list as short as possible.

When you are delegating, have some sort of plan so your delegation isn't haphazard and remember that the responsibility still lies with you for getting the job done well and properly.

Remember that when you delegate something, someone may find a better way of doing it so you may learn something yourself or they may end up doing a better job than you.

Giving instructions

When you are delegating, ensure that the instructions are clear. You should make sure the person you are delegating to knows what is to be done, when it should be finished by and to what degree of quality or detail.

Ask people to provide you with a progress report of how things are going. You may like to give them a cushion deadline where you have some extra time set aside just in case.

Consider delegating what the actual objective is rather than the procedure. People can get behind an outcome much more than they can the methodology for doing it.

Ensure you delegate the authority along with the responsibility. It can be really frustrating for someone to be delegated something to do but have no authority in the process. Give them the decision making power within boundaries you feel comfortable with.

Spread the delegation around. Don't always give things to the most able person and ask for feedback on how the tasks are going.

To help get the person going, ask the simple questions, "What else do you need to get started?" It's a great way for them to either tell you what help they need or for them to realise it's time to get a move on!

Tip: Remember these three important factors and make sure the person you are delegating to knows what is to be done, when it should be finished by and to what degree of quality or detail.

"Integrity is the most valuable and respected quality of leadership. Always keep your word."

- Jim Rohn

Change management

In the business world, there is a constant flow of change. In fact, some industries are all about change. We have new technologies, restructures, new team members, new board members, changes in governments, new laws etc. Managing people through change is often difficult, especially if they know a change is coming but they're not sure what it is yet.

The biggest issue with change management being conducted poorly is lack of communication. People really just want to be kept informed for a start. The grapevine (the unofficial communication line) carries a majority of truth but is not often reliable. Companies that provide transparency are more likely to maintain a sense of loyalty in their staff.

Many people are resistant to change. In fact you may have resisted some change yourself. If change is resisted, it's normally something that has to be accepted at some point so you may be putting off the inevitable. As a leader, if change is coming, you need to get on board quickly so you can assist your team with getting on board.

A great book on change is "Who moved my cheese?" by Spencer Johnson. The book is simply a story about two mice and two people who are used to having cheese in the same place available. One day the cheese diminishes and eventually is gone altogether. The story follows the characters and their attitudes to this change. I highly recommend you read the book.

There are several messages in the book including the following:

- Change Happens. Accept the fact that change is part of life and things will change. We can't expect all things to remain constant or there will be no progress.

- Anticipate the change. Keep your eyes open. Things don't stay the same for very long. Be aware of what's going on around you and be prepared to move again. Don't allow yourself to be blindsided and catch you unaware.

- Monitor the change. It is hard to always be on the lookout for constant change – especially after change has just happened. However, monitoring the change to make sure it isn't going to change again without you knowing is important – it's like an extension of anticipating the change. Just keep looking and seeing how it's panning out.

- Adapt to change quickly. The quicker you adapt, the quicker you can embrace and enjoy the new change. Old habits and attitudes need to go when the new change comes in. If you cling onto these old habits and attitudes, you just make things difficult for those around you and yourself. You don't want to be the one who is always complaining about it not being like it used to be. When you consciously accept change, you find you just then get on with it and you can move on. It's only when we refuse to accept or just ignore the change that we find ourselves constantly 'swimming' against the tide – and it's really hard work!

- Move with the change. This requires effort and means that you run with the new change. You actually move in the direction of the change. Be a mover, not a passive spectator of change.

- Enjoy the change. Once it's happened, take time to enjoy it. If it's a new person moving in to a role – enjoy the fresh experience. If you have a new process to perform, take time to enjoy the new opportunity etc. If you keep being obstinate about the change you will never be able to enjoy it and the rest of your life. If you don't embrace the change and get the blessings of it, you will look at change as the enemy and something that will steal whatever enjoyment you could have had that the change could bring.

- Be ready to change again. Positivity feeds on itself. If you have the right attitude no matter the circumstances you will enjoy life so much more. So if change is running away from you, catch up to it and change your attitude towards it and enjoy life!

Embracing change

In order to help yourself and other people move with the change you can focus on the following:

1. Seek to understand the change
2. Make a conscious decision to embrace the change
3. Identify the benefits of the change
4. Link the change to your own personal values
5. Accept that others may resist or struggle
6. Explore the perception of others about the change.

Let me explain a bit more about each of these points and they can assist you in accepting and embracing the change and how you can then help others to do the same.

Seek to understand the change. For us to accept change, it helps to fully understand what it is and what it means for us. So many times, people assume what a change is and find it is something very different when it happens.

Consciously accept the change. When you make the decision to accept the change, it allows you to move on and move forward. Until you decide to accept the change, you will be using up a certain amount of energy in resistance to it.

Look for benefits in the change. Sometimes it's hard. If the change is a reduction in salary due to cut backs, you may find it difficult to find benefits. One may be that at least you still have a job. Finding benefits helps to focus on what to look forward to as a result of the change. It gives you focus and a positive link.

Link the change to your personal drivers or values. If you can find a link in the change that matches your own personal drivers, again you will find a very good focus to put your energies into.

Accept that others may struggle with the change. If you can change or move with the change because you have identified certain benefits or established some good links, it doesn't mean that everyone else has. Be patient with others and accept that it may take a while longer for them to get on board.

Ask others what they are thinking about the change. Explore options with them. Ask them how it will affect them, have they identified any benefits themselves.

Help others accept change

Once you have managed all this for yourself, it's time for you to help your team do the same. You may like to run a short workshop to help them go through these processes themselves and help them manage this change process. Help them identify benefits, link to personal drivers and understand the change.

Sell the benefits of the change to others and if you feel like it become a champion of the change. Be someone who is an example of the change benefits and what they mean.

Part of the leader's role is to manage change and help others through it and the best way to do that is to become converted to the change yourself. You may need to take some time out and follow the six steps above so you can internalise the correct attitude and be ready to help others experience the same for themselves. Remember the longer you resist the change, the less happiness you will find.

Tip: Focus on the benefits of the change and link your personal drivers. Once you are committed, you are better placed to help others.

"I am personally convinced that one person can be a change catalyst, a "transformer" in any situation, any organization. Such an individual is yeast that can leaven an entire loaf. It requires vision, initiative, patience, respect, persistence, courage, and faith to be a transforming leader."

- Stephen R. Covey

Set clear expectations

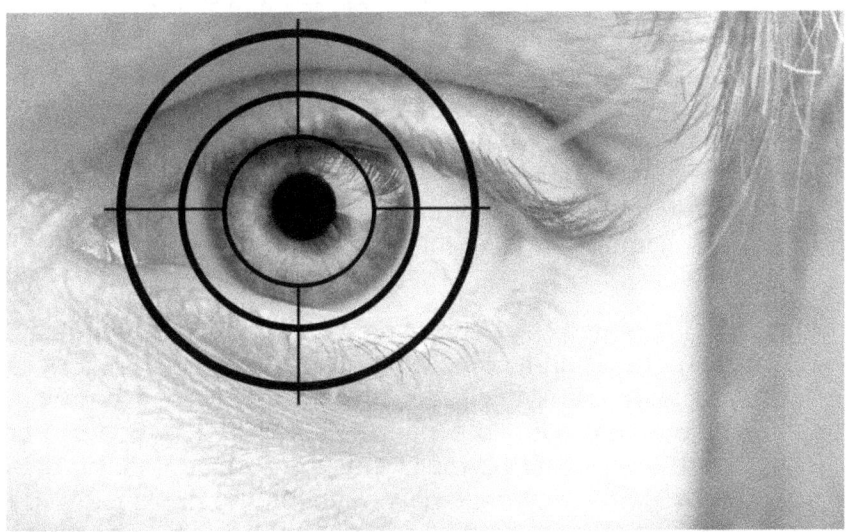

One of the big issues that people have with their managers is that they claim their manager changes their mind or moves the goalposts. All frustration is born out of unmet expectations. Not just people with their bosses. ANY frustration is as a result of not having your expectations met. If you expect one thing and get another, you get frustrated (unless of course your expectation is exceeded)!

So, think about your communication with your team. Make sure it's clear and concise. Avoid ambiguity unless you intend for it to be there. Remember the components for clear delegation; what is it you want done? When do you want it done by? To what standard and quality should it be completed? If you are clear, neither party will be disappointed or frustrated.

Consultation

One area of clear frustration is in consultation. If you are asked for your opinion on something and then someone totally ignores you, you wonder why they bothered asking you in the first place. Well, your team will be the same. If your intention is to gather opinions but make the decision yourself then tell them so they don't get the wrong idea.

There are three types of consultation, namely:

- We'll discuss – I'll decide: This is where you talk things over with your team or the stakeholders involved but you retain the entire decision making process. You may canvass their opinions and they may influence your ultimate decision but you may still run with your original thoughts. In this case, you must tell your people at the outset that this is your intention. Let them know that you will ultimately make the decision but you value their opinion.

- We'll discuss – we'll decide: As the phrase suggests, this is decision-making based on true consensus. Here you work with your team to come up with a decision. Ensure that everyone has their say and is heard. For those who don't normally say a lot or contribute, give them some advance notice about the topic because they may be the kind of person that likes to think things through before talking. As a leader you may miss out on some valuable insights because of this fact.

- We'll discuss – you'll decide: This version means that you are inviting others to consult with you but you're not offering to make the decision for them. You may offer advice and ideas but the decision is theirs and they have the responsibility too.

Brainstorming

Gather your team's ideas through brainstorming. You can do this effectively with a whiteboard or flipchart. You can pose a question or a statement and then canvass ideas. While brainstorming, it's important not to throw anything out to start with. The minute you shoot someone down for an idea, everyone will feel uncomfortable because they don't want to get the same treatment.

Your goal here is to get everyone to contribute as much as possible. You can reduce the list of ideas afterwards. You can improve your chances of fresh thinking by using methodologies like LEGO Serious Play or an external facilitator. Use open and searching questions to get people started and thinking.

Always provide feedback to your team following their involvement. One of the biggest complaints about managers is that they ask for their team's opinions and thoughts and that's the last anyone hears about the subject. Ensure you feedback to them the result and updates along the way. They will appreciate it.

Clarification

One of the simplest errors in communication is the failure to clarify. It's a great practice and easy to do once the habit is formed. Train your team to clarify with you to ensure they are clear with your instructions. Help them see the importance of clarification by doing it yourself. If there is any doubt, check. It only takes a minute and can save hours of wasted time and effort or correction of mistakes and embarrassment in the long run.

You want your customers to have a great experience and you don't want them to experience errors or problems. Many of these can be overcome by having your team clarify with them their requests or needs. If they get used to doing it with you, they'll do it with the customers and vice versa. Highlight mistakes that are caused because of the lack of clarification. Show how easy it would have been to avoid the error if they had clarified.

Tip: Get used to asking clarifying questions. Train your team to do the same. With clear expectations and less ambiguity, you'll have less disappointment.

"If your actions inspire others to dream more, learn more, do more and become more, you are a leader."

- John Quincy Adams

Power questions and power phrases

Barrack Obama as US President once stated that one of the key skills effective leaders of the future will have is their ability to ask powerful questions. It is true that transformational leaders – those that wish to transform change in others ask innovative and searching questions and lots of them. So whether it's a question or a phrase you want to share with your team, consider how you can make it powerful.

As an example, if one of your staff members is consistently late to work, you may be tempted to ask a factual question such as, "Why were you late today?" There's nothing wrong with that question but it isn't very soul searching. You may get a factual response like, "I overslept" or, "I missed the bus" but that's about as far as you may get. Consider the alternative, "What impact do you think you being late has had on the rest of the team?" With this question, you have suddenly transformed the emphasis away from the reason they may have been late to the impact it has had on other people.

A powerful question is one that makes us or the person we ask it of to think or to search our soul. Consider the self-posed powerful question, "Why do I do what I do?" Occasionally, we should all take a minute and ask ourselves this question. "Why do I do it?" It helps to focus our efforts and remind us as to why we're in business.

We often get so wrapped up in everything we do that our tasks meld into one and we can get caught up in mundane tasks very easily, so consider the important question, "Is what I am doing now the most important thing I can be doing with my time?" Wow! What a great question. In fact ask it of yourself right this moment. What's the answer? Is there something else you could be doing that would have more impact in your role or your life right now?!

So consider a few powerful questions or phrases you can keep and refer to with your team so that you can help them be more likely to understand a deeper purpose or reason for doing something. Here are a few other power phrases and power questions you could consider using:

- Why do we do it that way?
- Would that behaviour be acceptable if it was your mother calling?
- Own it!
- Make this one really count.
- Imagine this is the last call you will ever take. How would you like it to go?
- What would make this perfect?
- What would happen if we changed this?
- How long do you think we could last without customers?
- What's the one thing you would change if there was no limit?
- What's stopping you?

Questioning is pretty basic in the communication cycle but we still don't always use effective questioning. It's true that open and closed questions are the basic types of questioning but there is so much more to communicating than that. When I ask my children how their day went, it doesn't matter if I ask an open or closed question; I still get a one word answer like "Stuff" or a shoulder shrug. One of the better ways I have found to get them to open up (which is what we want from our team members) is to rephrase the question in to more of a request, "Tell me about your day". It gives them less of an option to avoid talking. Try it out. Use "Tell me about that conversation" or "Tell me about that customer" rather than "What was that conversation like?"

When you are talking with your team members, be ready to challenge them. It's part of your job to help them find the understanding as to why things are done, why customers need what they do, why your business exists. We need to move beyond the superficial and get inside the reasoning so we are all more connected to the business and the customers. You know this has happened when your staff say things like, "Our customers", "Our business" and "Our culture" rather than the third person versions ("The business", "The customers" etc).

Tip: One of the key skills that future leaders will have is the ability to ask powerful questions.

"Let him who would be moved to convince others, be first moved to convince himself."

- Thomas Carlyle

Some final thoughts

As a leader, there are many aspects for you to put your energies in. Know that you will never know everything and there is always something to learn. No two situations are identical. No two staff members are the same. The more you know, the more techniques you develop, the better equipped you will be in dealing with your staff behaviours, leading them effectively and building the confidence necessary to be an excellent people leader. Here are some other aspects to be aware of.

Managing your time

Time management or personal effectiveness is an on-going skill to be learned. Even though we have heard lots of tips on this subject we still struggle to implement good practice. Everyone has exactly the same amount of time in a day. Yet some people always seem to be rushing about, behind schedule in their jobs and lives, while others are calm and unhurried and seem to get the same amount of work done in less time.

Time management will help you organise your time so that you are spending more time working on activities that matter and less time on activities that don't. It can help you become a more effective leader, and therefore more valuable to your employer and your team. It can also help you reduce your stress levels.

One thing you can do to identify where your time goes is to set up an activity log. This is where you record all your activities over a period of time (such as one week) and identify exactly what you spent your time on. This helps you accurately identify some of the time wasting activities.

Next make a 'to do' list. This is a list of the important things you need to get done. Then prioritise this list. Identify what is important and what is urgent. Of course do the important and urgent things first. Try to avoid things becoming urgent as these activities are the ones that cause you to be under the most stress. If you can plan in advance, then you can avoid a lot of things becoming urgent and get them complete before they become so.

Set deadlines for things to be complete and allow a 'cushion deadline' which means you actually have some spare time in case of an unexpected interruption. Avoid making your deadline the same as the *actual* deadline.

Grouping and interruptions

One technique that can save you time is to group similar activities together. If you have a few phone calls to make, schedule a time to make them one after the other and get into a 'groove' as you make the calls. If you are reviewing a report from a team member and you find an item that needs discussing, don't go to them immediately. Finish reading through the report and make notes on all items to discuss and do them together.

It's also important to manage your email responses. Consider turning off the email notifier and schedule specific times in the day to look at your emails. Unless your job requires you to answer every email immediately, plan times to read emails in batches. You'll find you have much more 'flow' going on in your work and that you are more proactive in your approach.

As a leader, you must be available for your team members when they need you. However, like any worker you need uninterrupted time to be able to get things done. If your door is always open, your team members will constantly be stopping by to ask you every little question that pops into their heads, and you won't have any uninterrupted time. The best way to balance your team members' need for your input and your own need for quiet time is to set aside specific times when your door will be open, or walk around your team's area in the office at a particular time every day. You might also set aside a time when your door will always be closed. There will be urgent problems that team members have to interrupt you with, but you'll find that they interrupt you far less often if they know you'll be available for them at a particular time.

Meetings

Running effective meetings is part of the leader's role. We have all been in meetings that have dragged on, not met our expectation or had no real ending. Some meetings can be very frustrating, especially if there appears to be no purpose or that the original purpose is lost.

Be aware that it takes a really good meeting to be better than having no meeting at all. If you take this view, you will avoid having pointless meetings or meetings for the sake of it. One really good way of keeping meetings short is to hold a 'stand up meeting'. This is a meeting where you have no chairs and everyone remains standing for the duration. People get uncomfortable really quickly in this setting and it helps people to move things along quickly.

Have an agenda for meetings. Let people know in advance what the purpose of the meeting is and allow them time to prepare their thoughts and any contributions. This is especially important if people don't normally say much. It's probably because they need time to consider their thoughts. If you give them advance notice, they are much more likely to be ready to contribute.

During scheduled meetings such as a weekly team meeting, consider having a short training session. This doesn't need to be long, perhaps just ten minutes. Organise someone to present something as a training slot. It could be a refresher, something new, or a topic that you feel everyone could benefit from. This is one way to continue to develop your team on a regular basis.

Be an effective meeting manager by keeping control of what happens in the meeting. Don't let things go off topic too far unless you plan to. If a discussion starts to diverge of on a big tangent, consider using a 'parking lot' idea which could be a flipchart where you record the ideas to be discussed later.

Always complete a meeting with action points. A lot of people record minutes which can be useful if you need an audit trail of what was discussed. Minutes are way more effective if you have SMART action points connected so you can measure the success of the meeting through action points assigned to relevant parties as a result. Allow the meetings to flow by avoiding putting people down that come up with ideas and thoughts of their own. Be respectful to them and encourage participation. You can limit participation by setting the expectation up front by saying something like, "We will only have time in this meeting to look at two or three ideas on the subject but we can table any additional ideas for a later meeting".

Start meetings on time. Don't punish the people who have turned up on time by waiting for those who are late. People will get the message quickly if you start when you say you will and also finish when you say you will also. If you have trouble starting on time, consider putting a fun thing or important thing at the front so people won't want to miss out.

Managing your boss

You may have mastered how to lead your team effectively but still struggle with your own boss. This is not uncommon and you are not alone. There will be times when you don't see eye to eye or when you feel like you are being dealt with unfairly. You may have unreasonable demands placed upon you or you may feel like you just don't click.

The first point here is for you to appreciate your boss's goals and pressures. Find out what they are measured on and what their pain points are. If you can make them look good or ease their pressure, they will have more time for you.

One way you can view your boss is as a client. Find out what their expectations are and work to manage them. If your boss were a client, how would you handle that relationship? You would want to have regular meetings, inform them of changes, look to provide solutions and communicate effectively with them.

Work out what is the best way to communicate with your boss. Do they prefer face-to-face, email or phone? Find out what they prefer in the way of reports and written communication. Do they like lots of detail or bullet points?

Tell your boss what you need. Be proactive in telling them your preferences and outline any resources you need to get the job done. Remember that you are not their sole focus, so try not to take all of their time.

Sometimes you manager will not be quick with decisions. You need to be able to communicate what you need in these circumstances. Help to sell the reasons as to why you need a decision when you do and the downside of delays. Avoid sounding like the doom machine though. Don't make everything dramatic or imminent as your boss will quickly tire of that behaviour.

The micro manager

If your boss is overly controlling or very involved in everything you do, it's likely that they need more confidence in you. Start off by asking for complete responsibility in smaller tasks and then work up to bigger ones. Prove to them you are quite capable. Make sure you deliver excellent work consistently and seek to build trust.

The indecisive manager

If your boss is vague or hesitant, limit the choices you give them and make a single clear recommendation. If you feel that things are vague, seek clarification to help you and them get clarity. Communicate your deadlines clearly and follow up.

The unreasonable manager

If your boss overloads you with work or fails to see what pressure you are under, organise a meeting to discuss the priorities and options for excessive work. Avoid sounding negative about what's asked of you and explain what problems may arise if you don't organise what's the most important priorities.

Overall, you want to be able to understand your boss and provide consistent good work. Help them to look good and be clear with them of your needs to.

The team charter

One way you can help your team to peer manage each other is to set up a team charter. This is a set of guidelines that says, 'This is how we work around here'. You could include areas such as:

- Conduct towards each other
- Dress code
- What to do if you feel uncomfortable
- Work ethics
- How to show respect etc.

Always include the team in setting up a team charter. Never impose the guidelines and also consider what the consequences are for those who break the rules. You'll find that the team will self-police these guidelines if they are agreed upon and visible and that consequences are followed up on.

When new people join the team, the charter is something you can discuss at interview stage so that they understand what is expected in your team right from the outset.

There are many examples of team charters available on the internet. You can pick up some great ideas on how to get started. Consider canvassing your team's views on the idea and help them understand the benefits of having one. It's a great way to iron out some of the on-going niggles in a team and will help save a lot of your time resolving issues that won't even need to reach you.

Derek Good Bio

Derek is an author, actor, presenter, facilitator, voice over artist, husband, father of four children and currently a director of LearningPlanet Limited which helps improve the productivity of organisations and the confidence of their staff through sales, service and leadership skills in bite-sized videos and short training modules.

Derek is a facilitator who works with leadership teams in LEGO Serious Play, TMI profiling, problem solving and strategy sessions.

He was previously the Managing Director of Rapid Results - a leading New Zealand training and consultancy firm specialising in contact centres. There he was responsible for spearheading customer relationships programmes and managed all the sales and communications functions for the business.

Derek has over twenty years' experience in general management in the UK and New Zealand market, is an Author of several books on leadership, coaching, sales, Return on investment, training activities and humour. He has also been a past winner in the Westpac Enterprise Auckland North Shore Business Excellence Awards and the TUANZ innovation award for Education.

Other books available from Derek Good

Return on Investment Made Easy by Derek Good & Craig McFadyen

Paperback: 108 pages
First Published: 2010
ISBN-10: 1452835993
ISBN-13: 978-1452835990

Coaching and Feedback Made Easy by Derek Good

Paperback: 82 pages
First Published: 2010
ISBN-10: 1453844384
ISBN-13: 978-1453844380

ROI: The sales person's secret weapon by Derek Good

Paperback: 56 pages
First Published: 2011
ISBN-10: 1463764634
ISBN-13: 978-1463764630

Practical Leadership by Derek Good

Paperback: 172 pages
First Published: 2015
ISBN-10: 1512311650
ISBN-13: 978-1512311655

Notes

www.ingramcontent.com/pod-product-compliance
Lightning Source LLC
Chambersburg PA
CBHW051338170526
45166CB00002B/864